The Brain Is the Ocean We Live In

A collection of lyrical reactions

Cătălina Florina Florescu

Solis Press

To **M**, my best creation
(Love is love is love)

© 2025 Cătălina Florina Florescu

Published in 2025 by Solis Press

All rights reserved. No part of this publication may be reproduced, stored in a retrieval system, or transmitted, in any form or by any means, electronic, mechanical, photocopying, recording or otherwise, except as permitted by the UK Copyright, Designs and Patents Act 1988, without the prior permission of the publisher.

The author of this work has asserted her rights under the Copyright, Design and Patents Act 1988 to be identified as the author of this work.

This book is sold subject to the condition that it shall not, by way or trade or otherwise, be lent, resold, hired out or otherwise circulated without the publisher's prior consent in any form of binding or cover other than in which it is published and without a similar condition including this condition being imposed on the subsequent purchaser.

ISBN: 978-1-917904-06-3

Published by Solis Press, England

Web: www.solispress.com | *X*: @SolisPress

Praise for *The Brain Is the Ocean We Live In*

Reading *The Brain Is the Ocean We Live In* by Dr. Cătălina Florina Florescu is like peering into the depths of a soul that mirrors our own hidden currents. This beautiful collection of autoethnographic poetry spans an amazing range of styles, metres, and topics, each piece deftly and delicately crafted. Rather than offering panaceas for fear or sadness, it provides waypoints for us to navigate our own emotional landscapes and create our own non-recipes for healing. *Professor Sam Illingworth – poet, academic, and founder of Consilience Journal*

Cătălina Florescu's extraordinary poems spark the reader's curiosity with their visual aspect and their verbal economy. They invite the reader to peer with the poet at the mundane and desires alike, deeply exploring, observing and naming absence, loss, displacement. Through the beauty and simplicity of her language, we come to relish her blend of realism and emotional turmoil. Her poems facilitate the encounter with another culture, the Romanian one, which permeates the English core, while also referencing important literary figures such as Sylvia Plath, J. D. Salinger, or Ntozake Shange. Imbued with linguistic fluidity and a distinct voice, her collection praises womanhood and its struggles: "If woman is fugitive that's / bc, like language she's never / fully done / necoaptă." *Clara Burghelea – poet and translator*

Right from the title, the audiences are invited to acknowledge that the space they are about to enter is reserved for a few people. Not to worry, though, the author welcomes in fact anyone who is willing to strive for something else. The more poems one reads, the more one realizes that they have a unique quality in the sense that they could be dismantled and reassembled at ease so that one word or one line or chucks of poems exist freely in the readers' intimate spaces. In the end, if lucky, the poet and her readers live in a multiverse where the original ocean seemed to have been the departure point in this wonderous journey. *Andra Rotaru – poet and journalist*

In one of the beginning poems of Dr. Catalina Florina Florescu's *The Brain Is the Ocean We Live In*, the speaker declares, "We fix ourselves a drink / when we can't fix ourselves," then wonders, "Why wasn't that the first lesson in surviving?" Indeed, as we move through this collection, we are confronted with poems that speak of the daily struggle to survive the lasting traumas of war and displacement, of facing tyrants who threaten our precious futures, of the pain of losing loved ones whose voices remain with us "like cicadas that refuse to let go of summer." Despite these challenges, the speaker learns to embrace her own vulnerability and self-awareness as a way of finding hope and strength. She says, "Contain your hurt / & hold it close to your heart." Florescu graciously shows that pain will "never stumble your growth," that to free a trapped sparrow, we can open a window, and to free us from despair, we can open our hearts with poetry—the kind a reader will find in this beautiful collection. *Faisal Mohyuddin – author of The Displaced Children of Displaced Children*

About the Author

Dr. Florescu has a Ph.D. in Comparative Literature with a focus on Medical Humanities. She teaches honors, community learning, undergraduate courses at Pace University, and graduate seminars at Stevens Institute of Technology. She is a working mother of a beautiful young adult son. She has published academic and creative books, including a memoir, a trilogy on breast cancer, a volume about Englishes and immigration, *et al*. Website: www.catalinaflorescu.com/ E-mail: fflorescu@pace.edu

Contents

Migrate	1
The Stubborn Sagging Kitchen Cabinet Door	2
My-grain	3
But Officer, the Body *Is* My Luggage –	4
A Picture's Testament	5
The Smell of Gas Reminds Her of Sylvia Plath	6
Seasonal (Sea, On)	7
Persistence	8
Lost Edge	9
Medicine Paper	10
The Beginning of Memories,	12
Vise: *Vise*	13
Birds	14
If Reality…	15
To Own Something Transitory	16
When One Is Missing…	17
Haiku	18
As a Woman,	19
Embodied Endless Column	20
To a Former Teen Who Is 20 Today	21
Like a …	22
If We Die Right Now	23
Childhood	24
-osis	26

Part(iciple)s	28
Lightness	29
Together, We Have:	30
Hurt Therapy	31
Another Reading	32
The Point of no Return	33
Museum	34
"Unsex Me, ..."	35
His Eyes	36
The Story of Two Yous	37
Sparrow	39
To the Girl Who Is in a Corner,	40
vs.	42
Sediments	43
Portrait in Syllables & Mixed Languages	44
Gossip	45
Genesis	46
Palm Sunday	47
Settling	48
Edited/Censored Libido (I Still Debate which One to Choose)	50
A Long Day	51
Home	52
A Lesson in Endurance Written on a Broken Shell	53
If ...	55
To Be or not to Be	57

It Is I Who Exists in an Inexistent Country	58
Hatching the Death Egg	60
Against Poetry	61
The Brain Is the Ocean We Live in	62
Metamorphosis (An Unfinished Poem)	63
No, (Mad)	65
Stuck in Time	66
Currently	68
Will	69
Knees	71
To Be Continued ...	72
Prescriptive	73
Memories, Inc.	74
Before Sunrise	75
Accumulated Sadness	76
Postcard from Dictatorship Communist Romania, ca. 80's	77
Anchors	78
I Hold Vincent	79
Brokenness	80
Visualization (Migraines for Beginners)	81
Sacrifice	84
Endnotes	85

kaí tí dén kánate giá ná mé thápsete
    ómos xechásate pós ímoun spóros

                                                    (Dinos Christianopoulos)

Migrate

Used for the first time in the 15th century
"Item this wyck dan thomas Astley departed to Abburgeyny with a migracion"*
    W. More saw it as a noun,
        which for grammar that means all the abstract and concrete things like
        living creatures
                                            places
                        ideas.

In the unseen, real laboratory of manufacturing words, the wordsmiths made sure that the word, no matter what, has the right amount of mei-†
        to change
        to go
        to move

                to assume multiplicity.
                        to   suggest   evolution.
                        to be   protean, liberating,   forever   ubiquitous.

And so, it ends:
on a political altar.

Wash your hands,
        Wash your face,
                You, begone!

We have roots.
        We *may* stay.

And so, it begins:
with the unknown
        migrating
                mei-
                      be.

---

* www.oed.com/dictionary/migration_n
† www.etymonline.com/word/migrate

The Stubborn Sagging Kitchen Cabinet Door*

Pain is a clear sign of evolution.

Without it,
we could not still
be here.

We fix ourselves a drink
when we can't fix ourselves.

Why wasn't *that* the first lesson in surviving?

Opposite,
the stubborn sagging kitchen cabinet door
sings her freedom.

Grafted in a suburban kitchen,
the tree of knowledge
delivers hope

of endurance.

---

* Originally published in Consilience. "Time" issue.

My-grain

Figure 1: Original artwork by Annabelle Krupcheck, commissioned by the author.

You are on a field.
You meet Holden.
       He is not a fugitive.
              He enjoys a loaf of rye bread.

You smile.

Inside of you
       There are grains and grains of pain
Piling up.
The sloosh that
Only you hear
Grows in intensity.

Outside, plain summer.
Inside, plain pain.

No plane of existence is ever the same.

You ask Holden to share his bread.
You start to chew
      your migraine.

But Officer, the Body *Is* My Luggage –

Said the woman carrying herself
Outside in the world
At dusk where sounds are
Resting,
Waiting.
My body is my luggage.
Inside it,
A map that leads to
All the journeys
I took or dreamed about
On Earth and far away too.
My body bleeds into yours, officer –
And rivers
And mountains.
My body has stories
Of longing to meet again
Those whom I lost too soon,
Of longing to meet
Those who will continue
Or intersect with me.
I would not want to live
My life any other
Foreign way.
This is my luggage:
If you open it up,
My body will occupy the airport
You will be forever mine.
In fact, it is too late to claim yourself
As one, after this exchange
You are inside my luggage.

A Picture's Testament*

This is the polaroid of winter moving
rapidly, forced to admit
__ a changing season:
We were here
The earth was holding us tight
__ a lovers' embrace
The sky was clear
We were enthralled
We knew of change
__ a transformation
We woke up
Thanking
Hoping.
We were here
We existed:
Let the image
Speak
__ Frozen in time.

....
* Inspired by "A Changing Season" by Sarah Parker. The poem is published in *Making the Unseen, Seen*, ed. by Kathleen Decker, High Tide Publications.

The Smell of Gas Reminds Her of Sylvia Plath*

She was only 30.

Cleaning the countertop,
another mother
saw her face
reflected in
all too familiar
domestic puppets:
a knife
a spoon
a fork
a National Latin Exam medal
an employer-of-the-month badge
a wedding ring.

A random bouquet of reflective surfaces,
slippery stages onto which
she still performs –
diminutively.

It has started to smell divine:
Peach pie and roasted pecans,
garlic & prosciutto plait
and the main dish: Sylvia.

What followed their 20's was
an intense churning:
"The woman is perfected.
Her dead

Body wears the smile of accomplishment,
The illusion of a Greek necessity."

Dinner is served!
Bring napkins.

....

* Originally published in Planoplyzine # 37.

Seasonal (Sea, On)

I am always down when temperatures swerve; I know they have to do that, that's in the script. I feel like a child who accidentally dropped her balloon and now I am chasing it. I see my son with a kite in his hand running. I see that clearly. I feel warm. The sky is here. It can't leave me. I go to bed full of images. When my retina is burned, I exist.

Seas

in the script. ▇▇▇ a child ▇▇▇
and ▇▇▇ kite ▇▇▇
▇▇▇ feel ▇▇▇ The sky ▇▇▇ . It can ▇▇▇ be
▇▇▇ my retina ▇▇▇ .

~~Seas~~on~~al~~

I am ~~always down when temperatures swerve; I know they have to do that, that's in~~ the script. ~~I feel like a child who accidentally dropped her balloon and now I am chasing it.~~ I ~~see my son with a kite in his hand running. I see that clearly. I feel warm. The sky is here. It~~ can't leave me. ~~I go to bed full of images.~~ ~~When my retina is burned, I~~ exist.

Persistence

When pain was unbearable,
Matisse painted with scissors.
It was unorthodox
but cancer had been a savage—still,
the artist's inner world refused to shrink – the irony!

When faced with adversity,
Close your eyes,
wander inside of you –
and cut the excess that
steals your happiness.

Lost Edge

The thing about New Year's
      promises
is that we make them
at the edge between
      a space that is disappearing
      & another that is not even there yet.

The morning after,
      Tired
      Thirsty
      Hungry
We return
to being
a dull, worn-out knife.

What we cut into
is a dismantling
      memory.

Medicine Paper*

As she opened her mouth
the adjacent church bells
began to chime.
It was not even the exact hour.

The wrist,
exposed
reminded her of what could have happened.

A moderator stuttered:
"This is ... a cir...cle,
we sh...are stor...ies –
a safe pl...ace."

On the left,
a defibrillator.
On the right,
A fire extinguisher and an ax.
On the table,
a shiny first aid box
and a pitcher of water.

A safe place indeed.
Customized.
A sanitized, state-of-the-art chain
of timed healing.

Adrenaline rushing through her body,
she opened the door
with church bells
interjecting:

"There is no place like home."

She picked up a fortune cookie:
Run inwards to your Morpheus.

---

* Originally published in Red Fern Review, the Summer 2024 edition.

The church bells rang for the third time:
Loud sirens started to gallop manically.

Was she saved?

If you know the ending,
swallow it.

The Beginning of Memories*,†

At one point, you say:
ya pam'yatayu: I remember.
It happened like this:

The train did not stop,
it went on going –
We waved.

Our bodies were moving
inwards
to save themselves
from the present.

It stopped to hurt.
We were on a field.
The sun was going down.
I looked at you.
You said:
Vy pam'yatayete tse mistse? Do you remember this place?
I shook my head.
You said:
Tut my zablukaly dodomu. This was where we lost our way home.
That's not possible.
Yes, you were small, you ran away, I ran after you, and we got lost.
 But, daddy,
 which life happened?

I see another train coming.
I stay.
My memories must return.

---

* Part of SHATTERED/*Artists Inspired by Artists*. Eds. Oana Cajal and Claudia Serea, New Meridian Arts, USA (2024).

† Originally published in Red Fern Review, the summer 2024 edition.

Vise: *Vise*

The purpose of a vise is
to hold metal when cutting

But in a doctor's office, you ask:
do you know what's a vise?

He looks at you worried,
amused & back to being worried.

You tell him, the pain
I feel inside my head

Is like a vise, that's all.
Vise is Romanian for dreams,

There I almost never hurt –
somehow, I am back in time

The linguistics professor teaches us
how one grapheme can change

The meaning of a word in a second
tare is different than *mare* & *sare*,

I look at the chalk how it invades the board
Playfully, knowing it will be erased,

Agreeing to dwindle; doctor,
why is there a vise inside my head?

Birds

the thing about birds
is that even when they quarrel
that feels like symphony.

if words were born out of
magic storytelling,
when did we lose command
of our voice?

as we are stuck,
birds migrate –
deserting us.

If Reality...

pains you
imagine you go to a bar
dimly lit
soft music
diffused voices
giggles like ripples

then what?
stay there
you imagine
things get real
close to real
better than real

what if ...?
no, that's for another time

or ...
yes?

I am here, too

I'd rather imagine.

when did I start to pain you?!

To Own Something Transitory

like our bodies
is to be at peace
that no matter what
we build
will be undone
in seconds
that the pain
is sooner or later
grafted onto
untethered memories
that the protean body
solid in photos
nearing its end is
a liquid heart
trailing
craving to be back home
this time for good
unharmed
preserved
in the infinite universe

When One Is Missing...*,†

1. Inventory:
   1.a. We need ammunition. To kill. To save our lives.
   1.b. We need blankets. It is getting colder faster in these places.
   1.c. We need paper and pen. To write. To make sure we lived through all this.

2. Love:
   We were eating breakfast when we were told to come and fight for our country. My daughter was small. Three days old. Her first day home. I was pulling my boots on. I kept my head low, I did not want to look at her, I went outside quickly. My heart kept pulling me back. I lit a cigarette. She started to cry. I had to stop listening at the door.

3. TV:
   3.a. The anchorwoman reads the ones who died.
   3.b. The anchorman reads the ones who died.
   3.c. The list goes on and on and on.
   3.d. The anchorwoman cries.
   3.e. The anchorman curses.

4. Dog:
   A dog looks vaguely at me. The dog smells the blood on my hands. I cannot wash away this nightmare. He yelps. For no reason, I start to count. It's freezing. I rub my hands. Blood pours out of them. The war *won*.

---

* Originally published in Consequence Forum.
† Part of *SHATTERED/Artists Inspired by Artists*. Eds. Oana Cajal and Claudia Serea, New Meridian Arts, USA (2024).

Haiku

Debilitating
migraine wipes out everything:
voracious monster

As a Woman,

you have the right
to remain
silent
anything you say
can and will be used
against you
in a court of law

where the laws that you made
will finally speak louder and louder
and you will pretend
remembering me

as a woman,
the court has always been
my body:
you have no right
to invade it

my parents
have no right either.

I came in this world
to devour freedom

in a court of law
that my body
defines

defying your
gravity

as a woman, I
have the right
to remain
silent

revoking your laws
destroying your court of injustice
becoming me.

Embodied Endless Column

To Brâncuși

When you left your country,
    What did you pack?
    Was it heavy?
    Tu?[1]
When I packed, I put so many books
I might have imagined
to wear them
to look presentable
to the New World.

When you left your country,
    How did the borders look?
    Did they know who you were?
    ți-a fost dor de casă?[2]
When I left, the airport was packed
& I was wearing reimagined cothurni—
in my head I had to be
uncomfortable when I was
crossing o *graniță*[3]
in my head I had to be
bigger than life when I was
landing.
    (There was a thud, Gaia did that.)

When you left your country,
    did you ever imagine that
    as a man you will reach eternity faster, or
    you did not care at all and kept
    touching the surfaces
    bringing them to *viață*?[4]

I am in my kitchen
birds are seated on
my endless column:
    infinite womanhood, and
    that means
    unpacking
    returning to marble, stone, wood:
    reclaiming
        originea firii.[5]

To a Former Teen Who Is 20 Today

   To M

When my son was in middle school
He came back home and said:
Great, mom, just great! He looked serious,
but there was also something comical in his delivery,
the two masks of our DNA forever intertwined.
You gave me birth when Hitler killed himself, and that
was hysterical, my body and its history dictate that –
It's also Jazz Day, if you care to look in other directions ... ?
& I was thinking of all the music that existed
in my Dobrogea, and the accordion that my sister & I
inherited from our mother's father,
how it breathed music into being.
*Tell your friends that when your mom-to-be
entered the hospital in Indiana, she wanted one thing only,
drugs, how American, don't you think?* & I resumed laughing.

I gave my son my healthy legacy of twisted humor:
convoluted, serpentine, heteroglossic –
it is mine just as much as
it is my father's coping with dictatorship
in a Romance-language country –
where when we laugh, we cry a bit, too,
So, take us whole, in our contradictory complexity –
& *dragul meu, tell your friends that sometimes
an origin story, like mine becoming mamă
means that history is not repeated, ci inventată
so that we pass on other legacies – and evoluăm,
looking with kindness at the foreigner.*

Like a ...

Post U.S. 2024 Presidential Election

The results came in so quickly
They were in a hurry
ashamed and wanted to be

        Out in the open
        Numbers did not want to be pointed at
        They wanted a clean, neutral state

Like preventable flooding
There was no raft readied
Like a band aid
Ripped fast and carelessly
The blood resurfaced
Like a landslide
Earth barely breathing, concrete exposing its fragility
Like a quid pro quo
We were told not to fool around

        Theater is catharsis
        But before that pity and terror
        And even before that
        (un)comfortable dialogues

But did we listen?
Like an eye for an eye

        & this is what the American people received.

If We Die Right Now*

If we die right now,
hold my hand.

If we die right now,
sing me a song:

*"Teche voda i mynayut' lita.
Oy, ne bizhy voda tak shvydko,
Shepoche yiy blakytna kvitka
Oy, ne bizhy, voda, tak shvydko,
Oy, zupynysya, khoch na khvylynku, –
Teche voda, ne zna zupynku,
Teche voda ne zna zupynku,
Hey!"* [6,7]

If we die right now,
we will become a river:
do not,
I repeat,
do *not* pack
anything.

We must go
almost as we came.

We must return
whole as water.

....
* Part of SHATTERED/*Artists Inspired by Artists*. Eds. Oana Cajal and Claudia Serea, New Meridian Arts, USA (2024).

Childhood*

Vasyl lays on a table.
You bring your mother's sewing kit.
You say, *We must be careful*.
I agree.
This surgery must succeed.
It will, it will, I say softly to the little girl.

You spend the entire day
preparing Vasyl for his surgery.
Vasyl is my father.
He is old and his cataract is progressing.
My dad broke his arm, and now Olena fixes it.
Her small hands gently touch my dad's body.
You will be fine, she tells him. *I will count to ten and then I will go.*
Go where? I ask her.
Nowhere, silly. That's what doctors do before they operate.
My, my, do I have to teach you so many things!
Ten, nine, eight, seven …

Olena, sweetie, go to bed!
In a minute, mom.
Now! You have school tomorrow.
A blast.
Another blast.

No, no, no, honey, I am sorry
just one toy allowed.
Olena looks at me.
She cries.
Take my dad, please.

....
* Part of SHATTERED/*Artists Inspired by Artists*. Eds. Oana Cajal and Claudia Serea, New Meridian Arts, USA (2024).

Another blast.
Olena is gone.
My dad is gone.
Around me, rubble.
And toys
So many toys –
The war becomes a memory
and we return to living.

-osis

For the Greeks the suffix
was a mark of a condition,
for the doctors
a state of a disease,
but what is health
stays a mystery
for we are never whole, and
that is another way to look at healthy –
for we are evolving
for we are suffering
for we are crying
for we are laughing
and these are parts of our whole.

When my grandma was born
she did not have a kyph<u>osis</u>
but her spine decided to follow
& mark her pain:
of losing her childhood to poverty
of losing her hope when widowed
of losing her only child, my mother
of losing her fair chance in life.

All were unseen conditions
that medicine couldn't treat,
but what my grandma did
was *spreading*
unconditional
sacrificial
selfless love –
daily dosage
until released
for good from
this fragile condition
we call
body.

My grandma, *Eufrosina*,
became her predicament:
Like her two mythological sisters, a charity.
Like her own name, a goddess of mirth.

Part(iciple)s

The dirty plates were waiting to be cleaned.
The bed was waiting for her warm body.
The dreams were waiting to wake inside her luscious mind.
Summer was waiting to offer her morsels of its infinite.

Many were waiting for her,
and yet
she was searching –

for a LEGO piece
to complete her set.

Lightness

Sisyphus decides
his rock
is a balloon
and flies away.

Together, We Have:

Strength
Chorus
Power
Colors
Voices
Embraces
Agonies
Departures
Wars
Goodbyes.

Turn the page:
is it blank
or a palimpsest?

Are you there,
represented
seen
singled out
forgotten?

Can you love yourself
and rebuild togetherness?

Smile,
the way back home
is always shorter.

Hurt Therapy

As in a map
whose topography is
fluid and ancient,

so much so that what
you see in a mirror is
your lost ones:

you retain the right to be you
inasmuch as
you have become them;
you are hurt
just as much as they were;
& you carry their pain
bundled inside your tears.

No matter
how often you hear that ubiquitous temptation
let it go
                          let   it   go
                                     let/it/go
you keep on walking
ignoring the sirens.

Letting *it* go
would mean
Losing your departed–
This time:
forever.

Contain your hurt
& hold it close to your heart.
Contrary to popular belief,
this will never stumble your growth.

Another Reading

Aside from being in charge, as in
on your own, the idea that one is

Born alone is foreign to me –
I was not alone, my mother was

There, the umbilical cord
is proof of our togetherness

I had company: so many babies
were born on the same day in March

I will not die alone either, I will
have memories to take with me

And a blank map where I will record
what I will experience instantaneously –

Along that infinite journey
I will have others to amplify me

The Point of no Return

except of the pain,
that stays
and never leaves me.

I went today
right into that point –
fragility wounded,
Again:

When
                                            Will
           I
                                                                                   Learn
     To
                                 Stop
               Hurting
                                                                                M
                                                                                   y
                                                                                   s
                                                                                   e
                                                                                   l
                                                                                   f
                                                                                   ?

In trying to speak up for myself
All I do is   uncover layers
                               upon   layers
of hurt
wrapped
                                                    in loneliness and agony:
No exit,
no return,
                                                                         baby!

Museum

The little girl calls for her mother repeatedly
in the backyard
And I think of drifts –
I think.
I can't be sure.
I need an x-ray for the moment
to confirm
That what I say
is the truth and
nothing
but the truth
in this improvised court of law
we call it body.

The girl dropped something.
I can't see what from my apartment,
but there are audio
markers of the fall
which I fill in as prescribed by
language, social interactions, history.

Mine?
Oh, well, many years ago
I started the descent into the underworld.
I kept falling
without reaching my mother.
I am left with memories
Which I fill in inconsistently:
My body is a museum
where my mind curates
installations of my
once
upon
a
time

& this is my truth
Un-whole.

"Unsex Me, ..."

What?!   *No*, William,   please, no!
Hop on that   forevermore train   of immortality,
go back in time   and let   Macbeth
confront her   man,   embrace
            her sex &   walk away,
dine copiously   with   uncertainty
and let   it   co-exist
with the conundrum   of being   a woman,
do not become   ruthless,   manly,   tough,   belligerent,   obnoxious,
insensitive,   greedy,   absent,   tone deaf,   vicious,
shall I go on?
                        Women will need   therapy
                to shake this   curse off,
we are   not   the weak   sex,
do not   unsex   us,
we are life,   and that   is
nurturing,   evolving,   layered,   vital,   beautiful,
exquisite,   flagrant,   selfless –
I could go on,   but,   Macbeth,   remember,
we   do   *not*   kill,
we love.   Start with   yourself,
touch   the skies   & breathe   acceptance
into being   – thank you!

His Eyes

In memoriam, to my father

Figure 2: Original artwork by Annabelle Krupcheck, commissioned by the author.

We took the wine from His hands
And drank it.
We took the fish from His hands,
And ate it.
But we wanted to see His eyes,
We wanted to touch His face,
And so,
We invented His image.

Is it real?

*Woman, our hearts
harmonizing different sounds,
our bodies overlapping ...*

I resume walking.

The Story of Two Yous

Figure 3: Original artwork by Annabelle Krupcheck, commissioned by the author.

Even Microsoft Word
signals a mistake
& suggests replacing *yous* with
you
yaus
yonus

but I refuse
or I linger
I am almost done with you

or lie to myself

I created you
when I was a teen
back home
close to the Danube River

I was in the bathroom
I was doing laundry
we finally had this fancy washing machine
my mother and grandma did not have to slave away

the machine was
dreamy
soupy
bubbly
overflowing
ebullient

you have the visual now, so, let's move on

I imagined a foreigner
being so close to me
I imagined love

the laundry machine finished its cycle
I left the bathroom

time passed
you become real
then, one day, poof,
you were gone

this morning
I washed my hands
& you came back

the water is in a glass now
I stay close by the Hudson River
I wonder if you want to be free

of my imagining
you

Sparrow

To Paul Laurence Dunbar

A day after the 2024 US Presidential Election, at 7:55am:

I enter the classroom. The windows are wide open. The outside noise is intense, and I can't hear myself and today, of all days, I must hear my sighs, and you must listen to my sighs, and I must hear yours and you must listen to your sighs:

> Do you see where I might be going with this?

A student says: "Professor, don't close both windows. There is a sparrow in the room." I left one open.

The student's name is Victoria. I think of Woodhull. I think now I know how history is deferred to be rewritten by constantly reminding us of our failures, of being rejected, erased or ridiculed. "How pretty you are..." where you replaces the noun lies, but today, of all days, you must tell the truth until these walls will crumble and fall and you and the sparrow and Victoria will be free.

> Stop spiraling. The students will enter the classroom. You are still their designated driver. At least until the end of the semester. You welcome them,

"Look, we have a sparrow with us. Look, someone stopped by our class today. We have a visitor. A foreign exchange species."

> But the sparrow is trapped. Now you see her pain.

I stand up and open the second window. She must return to being a weaverbird, that's what is written on her birth and death certificate. Not her name, date of birth, country of origin. But her communal purpose.

"Professor, I think the sparrow left us. I can't see it. I can't hear it." You nod, but it's a disembodied feeling.

Why don't they become your designated driver? Deservedly, nests are for birds for they use nature to resist our tricky hospitality:

> "... we ...
>
> With deadened heart ...
>
> know our loss ..."

To the Girl Who Is in a Corner,

After all these years,
waiting for me to react:
Îmi pare rău.
It was a history class,
in dictatorship Romania,
you got a bad grade
you thought it was not *right* –

The word like the reality it was
vaguely mimicking
was tricky and slippery,
but you did not know,
you were a child in middle school,

You had no idea what it means
to camouflage,
to create identities
like a deck of cards,
shuffling & shuffled
to fit contexts
to save you –

You were a girl developing
in a country that was not free
learning about history
in a textbook that was doctored
and the teacher put you in a corner
simply because you wanted
an explanation,
a second opinion,
another look,
But she decided your voice
could attract other & become a plurality,

So, she played the censor role
quieting down any rebellious voices,
although at that age you wanted
to know why you got *that* grade,
you thought it was a mistake,
instead, you would come to learn
that to say sorry,
to assume responsibility
is an act of courage –

& breaking character is
not an option for history
because it wants its role
as indicated on the playbill,
therefore, you will be sacrificed
without anyone feeling
sorry, guilty, or even
human –

You will have to wait,
the applause will come
cascading, and you will look at the girl,
take her palm in yours,
and leave the stage.

VS.

Hemingway is credited for having written the shortest story in literature.
I'm sure there were women whose sighs were way more intense and powerful.
But they were never properly recorded and archived.
Hence, there is no proof.

Anyway, I am aware that you are tired.
So, let me simplify.

Hemingway's story goes like this:
"For sale: baby shoes, never worn."
Here is mine:
"Unruly, love and live."

Sediments

of the past pains
shaken, they dissolve
in a liquid
that you drink
in lieu of a treatment
because the protocol for hurt
is eat leafy greens
exercise
and retreat in the crowd:
be one with what moves
because the protocol for hurt
is the sunrise.

Portrait in Syllables & Mixed Languages*

> *i found god in myself & i loved her/I loved her fiercely (Ntozake Shange)*

Ive never been good at cooking,
& here i am: mixin' ancestries and languages—

Romanian in itself is an adulterous Romance language
full with words from others

bc others have overstayed their welcome: Romans, Turks, Russians
and others came there like a river carries its mud and sorrows

or maybe
I dunno, maybe, bc the country's compass doesnt turn Romance
left and right
and up and down.

We let travelers, *străini,*[8] flâneurs
be with us & offered them our proverbial

pâine cu sare.[9]

Which reminds me that I've started cookin' smth,
no idea what!
I move backwards as foolproof mnemonic device:
and I remember that i was cooking

myself, reinventing,
er body does that – the last, desperate shot at fame,
only IDC,
fame is no biggie for me.

I need to make sure that what I do does not ever
erase my birthmark:
it's not a burden of being white but of being (a) woman
who fights with God and his alleged apple.

But maybe God is a woman who wanted to cook a pie
turned her head for a split second and saw a bite into
a fallen apple.

If woman is a fugitive that's
bc, like language, she's never
fully done –
necoaptă.[10]

---

* Published in The Blue Nib # 43.

Gossip

You know how people are –

He stopped and looked at him.
They will speak.
That's what they do.
People speak.
All the time.

We can't seem
to want
to stop
to speak
All the time.
That's what we do.

He was wiping his face.
Is it better now:

Bare?

Genesis

Gaston Bachelard once mused:
"What is the source of our first suffering?
It lies in the fact that we hesitated to speak.
It was born in the moment
when we accumulated silent things within us."

A woman enters –
and words become beads.
She makes a necklace:
first
lies
accumulated.

Bachelard has no idea
that what was once silent
now is in flux:

Women flow peacefully.
They were
born
to speak.

Palm Sunday

Pentru tata de Florii

When I was a girl, my father gifted
me delicate, elegant freesias,
as a young woman, I told
him I would leave Romania so,
he handed me a fifty-dollar bill
– we were in the
living room, it was the place
where my father & I watched too many
soccer games, just the two
of us because no one else
cared about soccer, but I
loved dad so much, I thought
he was bigger than life
because he was funny and kind
& when the dictator appeared
one last time on TV and the image
became static, my father and I exchanged
glances silently: neither he nor I
knew that in that liberating
December 1989, I would
leave & he would also pack
his things and move close
to the Black Sea, where Ovid,
the exiled poet & my father
both died longingly.

Settling

Figure 4: Original artwork by Annabelle Krupcheck, commissioned by the author.

All my life
I bent my waters to fit
small, dirty, inconvenient
containers –
Some were mine:
drop the pointing fingers!

Yesterday,
by the water,
I wanted to dump
all of it
and start anew

But I realized
that I am
full of muddy waters
that I like
sediments
that I can't
ever allow to erase
myself.

I am settling –
Finding the light and holding it tight.

Edited/Censored Libido
(I Still Debate which One to Choose)

White as in hospitals.
White as in classroom walls.
White as in this hospital gown.
White as in neon lights:
in hospitals.
in schools.
(*I feel a light déjà-vu.*)

Where I teach there are no windows.
Prisons. Panopticon. Foucault.
(*Is this part of the same poem?*)

Should I be thrilled that today I had to wear my blue mask while getting ready for a pap test? Should I be happy that its blue color interfered with the all-white theme:
walls > gown > examination table paper?
(*This is when I switch moods. Luckily, this applies to grammar, too. Phew, I'm saved!*)

These are rhetorical questions.
(*Seriously??? You lost it here. Big time.*)

White as in a blank note.
(*Listen, if you are alone, invent your Galatea. Let words return to sounds and sounds to movement and then let serenity cover us all eventually.*)

A Long Day

I went for a long walk
and reached the end
of Earth.
It was
full with
rinds
and I
wanted
to bite into one
you know
just for fun
or thirst
or maybe to pass
the time
because it was getting close
to bedtime:
I needed to feel
something
on my tongue

Home

Dear mother, I am   here studying & I am   studied. The grades are great, the days, long, the nights,   exhausting. I know you   think of me. I could FaceTime you easily, but it is
too hard.   **I am homesick.**   I wanted to see you this summer.
At school, they said   to defer any   non-essential international travel.
                         I thought
                                                I was   back
                         in 2020
                                        when we had
                         to stay   indoors.
               The difference is huge. That was a   virus.
This is something I can't   comprehend. You were there playing with me board games   when the internet was too unstable, replicating our fragile lives.   I remember one day how our neighbor was so scared and how you slightly opened the window   to talk to her &   breathe.
We were this   close to forget   how to breathe together, how to share   the same space, and today I   howl, imagining moons above my head, spinning faster & faster   out of control, like
I feel   inside.
                I do not think seeing you is non-   essential. I do not
think
                         eating my favorite foods is
                 non-   essential. I do not
think
                         hugging you is
                                           non-essential.
I feel heartbroken. I need you to know.   You probably knew. I did not burn the chicken   last time I cooked. It was   delicious.   I burned my fingers. I did not   cry. That felt redundant, non-essential.
I should have,   right?
What's happening   to me? The phone's screen saver is of   us smiling.
That seems so distant. Time is not a construct. I want to build an airplane.
I want my body to have wings. I want you to be   close.

Love,   your
daughter.

A Lesson in Endurance Written on a Broken Shell

Figure 5: Original artwork by Annabelle Krupcheck, commissioned by the author.

Asclepios wanted to heal

                                                                                                   humans,

more than that,
    he wanted to bring
    the dead from the "other" world,
but Zeus was terrified
                the former would make humans   immortal,
so, he did what he knew best,
struck
Asclepios
with
a
thunderbolt.

But,
like all miraculous, out-of-this-world entities, something
                                                                                    remained
after him:

a bright caduceus,
two twisted, yet   ecstatic snakes,
and our wonderous

shadows.

If ...

Dedicated to poetry

If Sappho did not
        exist
as poetess
              in fragments,
if her body-qua-poetry stayed full,
            without sparagmos
we would not
have continued
to come up on any stage
centuries after centuries
            after,
and heal her
and maybe heal us,
            too.

If she were not a poetess,
we would have stayed
            broken:
full of all parts
but deeply,
irrevocably
            unfixable,
            drifting.

It is because of Sappho
that we resist
the bad,
the terrible,
the convenient amnesia,
the forced silence,
the violence:
    We are
    Never
    To be ignored
by what is written over our bodies.

At the end of any day
great or awful,
some women stood up
and continued their marches
        flagrantly fragmented
that is,
undefeated
because
when one woman's body qua fragments
still *exists*
after centuries of aggression
that is called
    poetry,
    which, in simple parlance, means this:

    the transference of bleeding pain
    into vibrations
    back to the oppressor!

To Be or not to Be

was a question that made Hamlet tremble,
whereas to be ignored and ridiculed &
to be told you don't belong
is a reality some people face
when mirrors forget their sole purpose
is to reflect and not distort realities —
still, today, having learned
surviving lessons from literatures
I know I am in front of you, joyfully
packing companionships forever freed from
a nu fi.

It Is I Who Exists in an Inexistent Country

When I first learned English
I was a middle schooler
in a country that existed on a map –
dictatorship Romania
Eastern Europe
Iron Curtain
Scarce food
Propaganda as a new forced skin.
The words that I remember from that time
Were simple:
Book, girl, love, and happy endings.

I had to relearn American English
When I came to the States.
The place was real,
It existed on a map –
Indiana
But then I also discovered that grafting a new identity
Would require more surgeons that I could have ever anticipated
And that recovery would be a long, irreversible process.
The words that I remember from that time
Were more complex than before:
Foreigner, womanhood, borders, and everything will be fine.

Time flies.
I opened a jar and took out samples from it.
I hold Sappho:
She was an invention of herself,
That made her exist in fragments,
That made us touch her brokenness.
Her language was full of words that now co-exist in many languages
Her way of breathing has been to borrow our lungs,

And so, I
Have decided to exist
In an inexistent country
That pleases no one
But myself.

It is time.
Time to let all of you go.

Hatching the Death Egg

In memoriam, to my mother

The woman is hatching
a hallow egg:
barely moving
she looks for
a bed
to die.
It's not the one where she made love.
It's not her mother's either.
It's her daughters'.

She stays there awhile –
hatching is
almost over.

The woman is
a child
playing
again
until the end.

Against Poetry

From waist down
we have grown wings,
collecting stardust.

Reading this,
she froze.

Inside a store
she was buying food for another week.
Time was of the essence:
the manager wanted to close the store and crush on her couch,
the cashier wanted to wash his hands to smell of lavender,
the almond flour wanted to have an affair with quinoa,
the sole Gala apple wanted to read bar codes of all imported detergents,
and she could not remember –

if her wings wanted
another fitting.

The Brain Is the Ocean We Live in

I.
Girl and a bowl of water
      The kitchen has a warm feeling,
            despite austere dictatorship.
      The dad guts a fish.
      The daughter enters: I just need a glass of water.
      She leaves the room.
      The dad yells: Come here! Now!
            A small fish is transported from the belly of the bigger fish to her father's bloodied hands to the daughter's clean palms. She looks with care at the little creature that convulses. The dad brings a bowl with water and places the little one there. He has always been feminine in his loving energy.

II. *Married woman*
            I left my Danube. I never felt anything for the Wabash River, or the Hudson, even for Dâmboviţa in Bucharest, before I had boarded a plane to look at the Atlantic Ocean how it divides pieces of land. Water became my blood. I am still learning how to swim, when to drink, which water is poisonous …

III. *Now*
      The woman knows that nothing in life should be fully explained.
      That everything in life must be undone by the brain where depths are vastly unknown.
            And that's how the story ends:
                    The brain is the ocean we live in.

Metamorphosis
(An Unfinished Poem)

Figure 6: Original artwork by Annabelle Krupcheck, commissioned by the author.

Forget Ovid,
or insects,
or any other recipes for guaranteed metamorphosis.

This is the last summer
when we are alive
as humans.

It is so hot that we have started our descent into mythology.
Everything after this is going to be:

splash,
baa,
moo,

Bam!
Bam!

When this is over
We will stay as one:

Unhurt by loss.

No, (Mad)

I have a non-refundable ticket
to meet Mary Magdalene
and tell her
to come with me in
Paradise.

What she lived
was negligently scripted
by an amateur.

Because of that
women became
no(mad).

In other words:
(But
why
would
I
give
you
the
ending
when
we
have
not
even
started
the
journey
properly?)

Stuck in Time

Figure 7: Original artwork by Annabelle Krupcheck, commissioned by the author.

When I was a girl
I could not hear what my mother was hearing:
the seashell horn was beautiful,
but empty.
Put it to your ear, my dear ... like this.
There was nothing.
I ran out of the door –
my ears muted
to mystery.

After she died
the seashell horn finally spoke to me:
She is here:
Listen.
She is stuck in time:
like a diamond needle on a vinyl
like airborne sound waves migrating to a cloud
staying here
in perpetuity.

When I left my childhood behind,
I knew only this:
if I did not let all waters fall too harshly inside of me
she and I
my mother and I
will continue to be –
vibrations:
sounds that keep on going
inside the never-ending
seashell horn.

Play.
Pause.
Resume the sound.
We are stuck
in time,

my son.

One day he whispers:
Mom, I can hear grandma
like cicadas that refuse to let go of summer.

Currently

The most impressive thing about *currently*
is that it's moving

        so

                                            fast

it does not have time to look back

        so

                fast

you do not even realize
we were

        done

to being
currently

                in the current

so,
stop

                                        running.

If you do not believe me
repeat after me:

Curro, *Currere*, Cucurri, Cursus
Curro, *Currere*,   Cucurri, Cursus
Curro, *Currere*, Cucurri, Cursus
Curro, *Currere*, Cucurri,   Cursus

You do not know what you are saying,
I know

I am

                                        aware

Look in front of you
Do you see yourself

                running?

That's you.
That's what you are saying

currently.

Will*

Nu-ți voi lăsa drept bunuri, după moarte,
Decât un nume adunat pe o carte,

        Arghezi wrote in a poem

                                      if memory serves

If not

at one point we must face
      mortality

We must look at our feet

                                      and
                                      remember

One day our steps will stop being
what we feel they are

                right
                now

Our shoes
from when we were small to old
all will have disintegrated

                                      Where
                                      How

We do not know

We will go barefoot
meeting 432 Hz music

---

* Originally published in Red Fern Review, the Summer 2024 edition.

The ears will follow our shoes
That much

we know

Without proof

                                        of existence.

Knees

I have been waiting for
       the rain
for days and nights
tossing and turning in bed
waiting
wanting
waiting.
The knees
       a clock
that dreams about
the rain droplets
       to bring us closer
under an umbrella
to kiss
to embrace
waiting
deferring to precipitate –

my body
ticking ...

To Be Continued ... *

Imagine a hand. It is in front of you
reaching out.
Imagine a pair of scissors
that cuts papers
anticipating
the next holiday.
Imagine an equilateral triangle
bearing the burden of sameness
knowing that that was possible only
in geometry –
That life is strife
and light
and poorly cut out shapes
and that you
of all people, *you*
are awake:

Imagine that.

---

* Published bilingually in Modern Poetry in Translation.

Prescriptive

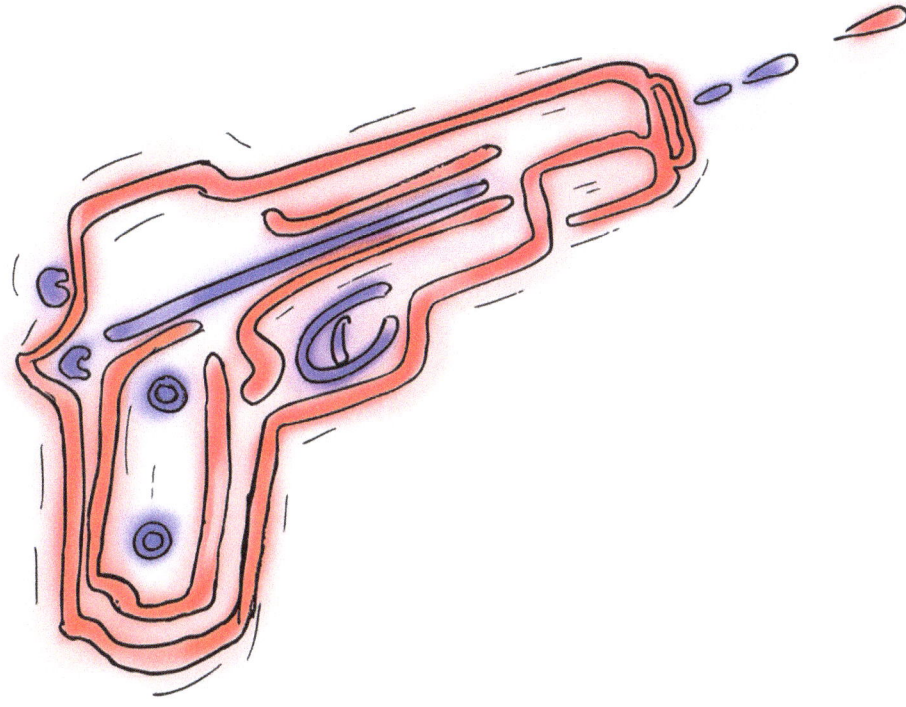

Figure 8: Original artwork by Annabelle Krupcheck,[11] commissioned by the author.

According to my dream last night
I died
an American death:
by gunshot –
a man –
in a neon lit hallway,
                        a total cliché.
Today I should read my obituary.

But here I am:
Coffee in one hand,
Quietly entering a new day.

Unless what I see
Is a broken record.

Memories, Inc.

With parents gone
I stare at that door
That stares back at me
& even says the same line:
Open me!

I almost did that
last night;
I went outside to smoke instead.

Look at my hands
Trembling:
How could they even hold
memories?

The C in Childhood has faded.
A mother explains to her son on their way back home:
It's not really gone.
You add what's missing.

I smiled
& everything was restored fully in me.

Before Sunrise

You open your eyes
and it's there:
The sun.
The tree.
The water.
You close your eyes
and it's there:
The echo of the sun.
The voice of the tree.
The touch of the water.
I do this every day:
While you sleep –
Said the bird.

It is the unseen
that trails majestically.

Accumulated Sadness

Her fist dropped,
now she looked like Marat –
as in the revolutionary.
In her hands,
a snowball:
somehow intact –
the melting refusing to happen,
just like everything she did.

It's possible that her being unseen-unheard-unloved-unappreciated-unwanted
to all have been a (cautionary) story of
accumulated sadness.

Or life,
and its die:
as in rolling.

(Don't stop.)

Postcard from Dictatorship Communist Romania, ca. 80's

Growing up, things were in black and white, but when one day I was gifted a kaleidoscope, I was mesmerized & would spend hours and hours close by the window, pressing that kaleidoscope against it, turning it ever so slightly, and sometimes, the illusion of colorful multiplicity would make reality slightly bearable, because to survive in black and white was to dissociate.

Anchors

I always thought that an anchor was nice but kept vessels in place and denied the end of their journey. Until my priest told me otherwise. Now I wear two. I go as I please. I stay as I please. I think I'm better. I find myself in deep, muddy, painful waters and then *someone* pulls me out of those churning, sensuous, relapsing moments. I have not seen their face. But whoever that may be, they feed me stories, images, sounds, smells, and change the diet of my thoughts, rerouting them. To my Good Samaritan, thank you. This is a true story. The only part that's missing is …

I Hold Vincent

It's funny how we met,
I was mapping my hurts
Matching them with sounds –
I was bleeding
& you listened:
Care,
Fully.

I picked you up.
You were tiny,
An ear
& inside of it
Full
Care.

Brokenness

why do we care about a broken femur
but turn our bodies away
from broken English?
the little girl asked her mother,
taking her tongue out,
just for fun, she claimed –
the mother replied, a broken femur hurts,
but broken English has no tongue:
a sign of sublime singularity.

Visualization (Migraines for Beginners)

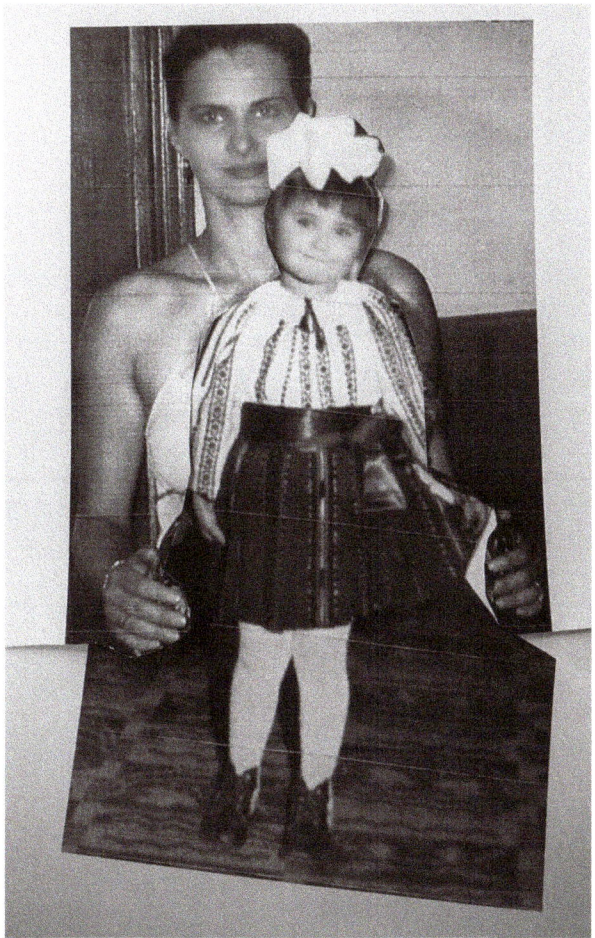

Figure 9: A collage with the author at distinct ages. Personal archive.[12]

It's not an album.
It's embodied.
It's not a story about you narrated by another.
It's a first, felt memory:
of you,
broken.

Unde te doare?[13] the mother asks.
Aici, the 5-year-old points to her head.
Cum te doare?[14]
The little girl has no idea how
to verbalize agony,
so, she gestures:
Two fists put together and banged against each other.

Try that.
They make sound,
you make sound,
but it's outside of you.

This is what the little girl feels:
the sound inside her head,
that loud beast!
*She wants to listen
to fairytales on their vintage record player.*

A 49-year-old woman confesses:
*All of a sudden, my head grows exponentially big,
But not in size, in weight.
Invisible to the other's eyes
But gnawing inside my head
and yet multiplying uncontrollably.*

*It's hard to put into words.
But you must see what I feel.*

*It's like I carry two bags,
I know their weight,
I feel comfortable holding them,
when, unbeknownst to me,
heavy loads are added.*

*My body, exploited, reacts as it descends into hell.
I lower myself.
I bend under pressure.
I drop the bags.
I stand still:*

My head has metamorphosed into cemented bricks.
I can't even gently move my head up or down
without feeling intense pain.

My own tears feel sorry for me.
They look at me,
refusing to come out fully.

I exist in the expanding land of pain.
But you see me whole.
Projected, we follow directions
and read together the woman's note:
It is I who must tell you how I feel
using a subject and a verb:
I suffer.
It is you who must listen.

Whenever I come back from a migraine episode
I dance like a lunatic,
I feel unstoppable.

I see the 5-year-old girl still terrified.
I take her tiny hands in mine.
Give yourself permission to be afraid:

Sunt aici.[15]

Sacrifice

To M

The bird,
wobbling
was handing me
her wing.

Is it for me to fly?
No, it is for you to write.

Endnotes

1. You (Romanian).
2. Leave Romanian as is, i.e., without translation.
3. Border (Romanian).
4. Life (Romanian).
5. Leave Romanian as is, i.e., without translation.
6. https://lyricstranslate.com/en/%D1%82%D0%B5%D1%87%D0%B5-%D0%B2%D0%BE%D0%B4%D0%B0-waters-flow.html and https://youtu.be/co2XflOFUYQ
7. Leave Ukrainian as is, i.e., without translation.
8. Foreigners (Romanian).
9. Bread and salt (Romanian).
10. In its literal sense, this Romanian word could mean "undone"/"unripe"; however, in a more evolved manner, it could also mean "mysterious," or "not fully revealed," or even, "you know, make an effort to know her."
11. Annabelle Krupcheck was Dr. Florescu's student when she took a course meant to stimulate conversations between the arts and writing. Later, professor and student would win a summer grant to focus on how writing can be translated visually, "Reinvented Emotions."
12. Photo statement: I could have used Photoshop and create a "perfectly" manipulated image, but instead I chose to pay respect to how a body feels inside when it's broken by a chronic, debilitating pain. I cut inside two old photos using scissors and then I joined them. In an unintentional tribute to Gordon Matta-Clark's 1970s series, this is my *Splitting, 1980–ongoing?*
13. Where does it hurt? (Romanian).
14. How does it hurt? (Romanian).
15. Leave Romanian as is, i.e., without translation.

www.ingramcontent.com/pod-product-compliance
Lightning Source LLC
Chambersburg PA
CBHW061224070526
44584CB00029B/3967